String Games

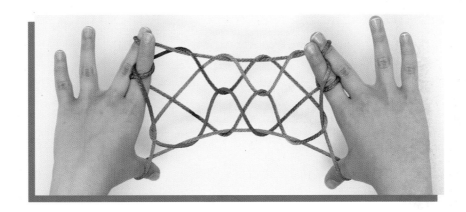

Richard Darsie

Sterling Publishing Co., Inc.
New York

This book is dedicated to the late Honor C. Maude (1905–2001). For over 20 years she visited islands all over the Pacific and personally collected over a thousand string figures, including many in this book. She played a significant role in rescuing the art of string figure making from oblivion.

Acknowledgments
A number of people played a part in the creation of this book. Talib and Olivia Huff taught me my first string figure about 10 years ago, unknowingly sparking in me a long-term serious interest in this art form. Great thanks are owed Mark Sherman, acting director of the International String Figure Association, who helped me learn many Inuit string figures. His many suggestions, and those of associate director Will Wirt, helped make the instructions clearer. Thanks go to my wife, Leslie Jones, who helped with preliminary illustrations, and to my sons, Brendan and Sean, for giving me a reason to be interested in string in the first place. — R.D.

The editor thanks Mrs. Baadh's Play Strings, Brisbane, California, for supplying many of the strings used in the photos.

Interior photography by Michael Hnatov. Page layout by Wanda and Kuba Kossak.
Edited by Isabel Stein

Library of Congress Cataloging-in-Publication Data Available

10 9 8 7 6 5 4 3

Published by Sterling Publishing Co., Inc.
387 Park Avenue South, New York, N.Y. 10016
© 2003 by Richard Darsie
Distributed in Canada by Sterling Publishing
ᶜ/o Canadian Manda Group, One Atlantic Avenue, Suite 105
Toronto, Ontario, Canada M6K 3E7
Distributed in Great Britain and Europe by Chris Lloyd at Orca Book Services, Stanley House, Fleets Lane, Poole BH15 3AJ, England
Distributed in Australia by Capricorn Link (Australia) Pty. Ltd.
P.O. Box 704, Windsor, NSW 2756, Australia

Manufactured in China
All rights reserved

Sterling ISBN 1-4027-0089-X

Contents

Introduction   4

Getting Started   5
What You'll Need   5
Some Definitions   5

Beginning Figures   13
Scissors   14
Jacob's Ladder   17
Walking Sticks of an Old Woman   21
A Chest Ornament   23
A Fishing Net   26
Lightning   30

Now Try These   33
Hina's Skipping Rope   34
Teniako's Bridge   37
Ten Men   38
Crayfish   42

String Figure Series   45
Mr. Umake   46
Crabs   53
Mt. Fuji   57

Figures for Two People   63
A Mountain   64
A Looking Glass   67
A Sting Ray   70

Catches and Tricks   73
Caroline Islands Catch   74
Cutting Off the Fingers #1   76
Cutting Off the Fingers #2   78
The Buttonhole Trick   80

Three-Dimensional String Figures   81
Two Mountains and a Stream   82
A King's Throne   85
The Howler Monkey's Mouth   88
A Butterfly   90

About the Author   94

Sources of the Figures   95

Index   96

Introduction

Almost everyone has heard about making patterns with a loop of string. The Cat's Cradle game has been popular with children for generations, but did you know that you can make a huge number of different patterns? Thousands are known, some very complicated.

Making string figures was a common practice among most of the tribal people in the world. It is hard for us in the modern world to understand the fascination that string figures held for these people. String figures once were associated with religion and mythology, and even magic and fortune-telling.

For example, the people living in Arctic regions believed in a spirit of string figures. The Navajo believed that the art of making string figures was a gift from Grandmother Spider, so they made string figures only during the winter when the "true" string weavers, the spiders, were asleep. The natives of the Gilbert Islands in the Pacific believed in a supernatural hero known as Na Ubwebwe, who served as a guide to the underworld and would not allow the dead to pass unless they could make a certain series of string figures with him. Among the Kwakiutl Indians, making a certain string figure served as a password for entry into a secret society. In New Guinea, string figures are used as a form of agricultural magic to help the yam stalks grow well and wind the right way. Making string figures gives us a small glimpse into the lives of the people who invented them and kept them alive for generations.

This collection includes many figures that are easy enough for beginners and some that are more chal-lenging, for more experienced people. In making string figures, one goal is to be able to work through the movements as smoothly as possible. A certain grace to your movements will develop with practice. You may some day want to invent your own figures. The most important goal, of course, is to enjoy yourself!

WHAT YOU'LL NEED

All you really need to make string figures is the string itself, the directions for making the figures, and a willingness to experiment.

You can use a store-bought loop of string, whose ends are glued together, or make your own loops by tying or gluing together the ends of a braided string, such as mason line.

Some figures in this book require longer loops than others. I've indicated with each figure the length of loop that is required to make it. Some figures can be made with any length of loop. Others need more specific lengths. The shortest loop used here is 36" long (91 cm), which is actually 72" of string (182 cm). Some figures require a 40" (102 cm) loop (80" of string), and a few need a loop that is 54" (137 cm) or longer (108" of string). Many toy stores sell cat's cradle strings. You can find other sources on the Internet.

SOME DEFINITIONS

The people who created most string figures had no written language. They learned string figures by watching other people make them. When Westerners (Europeans and Americans)

started visiting and studying these people, they wanted to describe how string figures were made, so a set of terms to describe specific positions and movements of string was developed. This made it possible to create written instructions, even for very complicated string figures. Learn the terms given below so you will understand the instructions.

String Position Descriptions

There are various terms that describe the position of the string loops on the hands. Every loop around a finger has a near and a far string. The near string is the part of the string that is closest to your face when your hands are held upright with fingers pointing upward. The far string is the part of the string that is farthest away (see Figure 1).

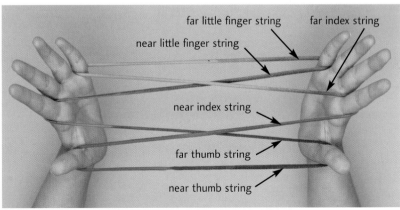

far little finger string   far index string

near little finger string

near index string

far thumb string

near thumb string

1. Names of strings.

Getting Started

Strings are identified by the name of the finger they go around. The left near index string is the one that is closest to you on the left index finger when first strung on the index finger, for example. But note: Even though a string may later be wound around another finger also, it is still referred to by its first wrapping around the finger, for example in Figure 2, the far index string is now closer to you, because it was shared by the thumb.

A section of string passing on the palm side of the hand from one finger to another on the same hand is referred to as a *palmar string*. In Figure 3, there are palmar strings on each hand.

A *transverse string* is one that runs straight across from a finger on one hand to the same finger on the other hand. See Figure 3 for an example. A transverse string that is a near string on one hand will be a near string on the same finger on the other hand as well.

If there are two loops on a finger, we say that there is an upper and a lower loop. The upper loop is the loop nearest the tip of the finger. The lower loop is the loop nearest the base of the finger; see Figure 4.

I use the term *MRL fingers* as an abbreviation for the middle, ring, and little fingers, when the three fingers do something together.

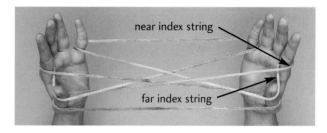

2. A string is named by the way it originally wrapped on the finger. Here the far index string is closer to you than the near index string.

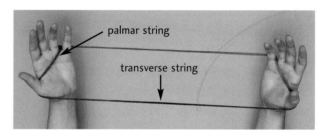

3. Palmar strings and transverse strings.

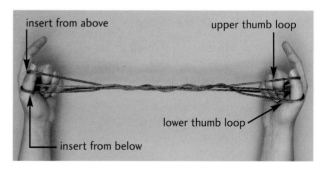

4. Here each thumb has two loops, an upper and a lower. Arrows indicate what *insert from above* and *insert from below* mean.

You may be asked to insert a finger (let's call it Finger 1) into a loop on another finger (let's call it Finger 2) from above (see Figure 4). *From above* always means you insert Finger 1 starting from the fingertip of Finger 2 and go towards the base of Finger 2. *From below* means you insert Finger 1 starting from the base of Finger 2 and go towards the fingertip of Finger 2. This is true even if Finger 2 happens to be pointing down.

String Movement Descriptions

Here I describe various common movements that occur in many of the figures in the book.

Return to position. The instructions often say to return your finger or your hand *to position*. This simply means to return it to the position it was in before beginning the movement, usually after picking up a loop.

Navajo loops. You will often be asked to navajo a pair of loops. In that case, there are at least two loops on the finger in question, an upper loop and a lower loop. To navajo the thumb loops, for example, means to take the lower thumb loop and pull it up over the upper loop and so remove it from the finger completely. Figures Navajoing 1, 2, and 3 show this procedure. You can move the loop with your teeth or with the fingers of the opposite hand. Navajoing may be done on any finger that has more than one loop around it.

Navajoing 1. Two loops are on each thumb.

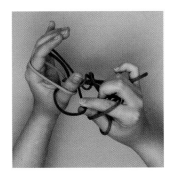

Navajoing 2. The lower left thumb loop is lifted over the upper one.

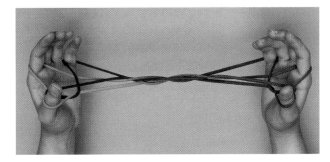

Navajoing 3. After the lower thumb loops have been navajoed, they are off the thumbs on both hands.

Share a loop. To *share a loop* means that at the end of a movement, a loop that had been around one finger will have an additional finger in it also. For example, in Navajoing 1 (page 7), the thumb and index finger share a loop.

Transfer a loop. To *transfer a loop* means that a loop that was previously on a finger (or fingers) is moved to another finger or fingers. Transferring implies that the finger that held the loop originally is removed from the loop. Unless the instructions state otherwise, the loop is transferred by inserting the new finger into the loop from below. (Sometimes you may be asked to transfer a loop by inserting the new finger into the loop from above, which results in a half-twist in the loop once it is transferred.)

Extend. To *extend* means to move the hands apart to pull the strings taut so there is no slack in them. The term *extension* usually refers to the final movement, in which the figure comes into view. The final extension is sometimes the most difficult movement in making the figure.

In the following paragraphs, I describe several commonly used openings and final extensions. With a little practice, you will be able to do them without thinking. Practice these openings until you can do them with ease, so you won't have to keep referring back to these pages when you start a figure.

Glossary of Openings

Position 1

Place the string on each hand so that the string runs across the palm in front of the index, middle and ring fingers, but behind the thumb and little finger and across to the other hand. Make sure the near thumb and far little finger strings do not cross between the hands. See figure of Position 1.

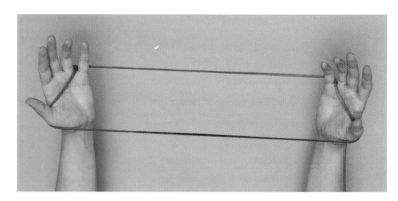

Position 1

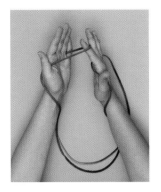

Opening A 1. Picking up the left palmar string.

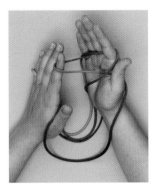

Opening A 2. Picking up the right palmar string

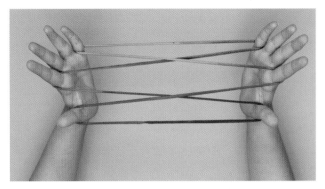

Opening A 3. The completed Opening A.

Opening A

1 Place the string on your hands in Position 1. Bring hands together and insert the right index finger from below behind the left-hand palmar string (see Opening A 1).

2 Insert the left index finger between the strings around the right index finger and put your left index finger from below behind the right-hand palmar string (see Opening A 2).

3 Pull hands apart (extend hands) to make strings taut (see Opening A 3). In this position, you have a loop around both thumbs, both index fingers, and both little fingers.

In Opening A, the string goes through its sequence of loops as follows: left near thumb string — left far thumb string — right near index string — right far index string — left near little-finger string — left far little-finger string — right far little-finger string — right near little-finger string — left far index string — left near index string — right far thumb string — right near thumb string — left near thumb string. It is a good exercise to see if you can understand and follow this sequence. Opening A is the most common method of beginning string figures throughout the world.

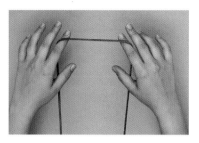

Navajo opening 1. Starting out: Loops hanging on both index fingers.

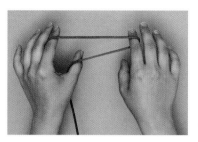

Navajo opening 2. Left thumb takes hanging right string.

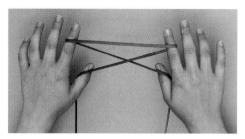

Navajo opening 3. Right thumb takes hanging left string.

Navajo Opening

The Navajo opening is another common opening.

1 With palms facing each other, fingers pointing upward, place the loop on the index fingers so that the near index string is short and the far index strings hang down (see Navajo opening 1).

2 Pass the left thumb under the near index string and to the right of the hanging right far index string (see Navajo opening 2). Catch the hanging right string on the back of the left thumb and return.

3 Pass the right thumb under the left near thumb string, under the left near index string, and to the left of the hanging left far index string (see Navajo opening 3). Catch the hanging left far index string on the back of the right thumb and return.

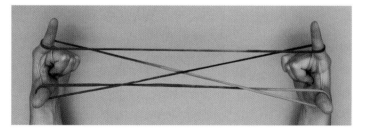

Navajo opening 4. Hands extend and thumbs rotate out to complete the Navajo opening. (Middle, ring, and little fingers don't have to be folded down.)

4 Extend hands to take up the hanging loop (see Navajo opening 4). This completes the Navajo opening.

Although it is called the Navajo opening, this opening is also used in some Pacific Island figures.

Note: The Navajo opening is not the same as navajoing a string (see page 7 for navajoing a string).

Index opening 1. Loop hanging on left index finger.

Index opening 2. The are two strings crossing the back of the index finger.

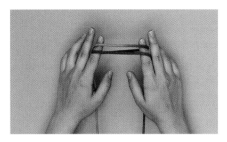

Index opening 3. Right index inserted from below into both loops.

Index Opening

1 Hang the loop from the left index finger with the finger pointing to the right (see Index opening 1).

2 With right thumb and index finger, grasp the far string of the left index loop, bring it towards you and wrap it once more around the left index finger, so there are two strings crossing the back of the left index finger (see Index opening 2).

3 Pass the right index finger from below under the long near index string and into the small left index loop (see Index opening 3) .

4 Extend hands (see Index opening 4). This completes the Index opening. You should have two loops on each index finger, with the near strings parallel and the far strings crossing each other.

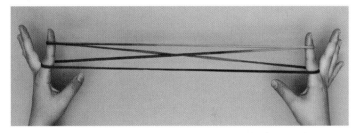

Index opening 4. Hands extend to complete the Index opening.

The Index opening is sometimes referred to in string-figure descriptions in other books as the Murray opening, named after Murray Island in the Torres Straits between Australia and New Guinea, where it is commonly used.

The openings described here are just a few of the many possible ways to start string figures. Several of the figures in this book do not start with any of these.

Displaying Finished Figures

When you have completed the procedure for making a string figure, there is usually a method for what is called the final extension of the figure. The Caroline extension is a very common method of final extension, but there are many others as well. Most figures will display properly upon final extension without any problem. However, many figures require some arranging or fiddling with the strings in order for the proper pattern to best be shown. Where this is the case, it is noted in the instructions.

Where to Start

The string figures given here are labeled by level of difficulty. Learn the openings and start with the easier ones. Don't be discouraged if you can't make a figure on the first try. You may have to make several tries before you are successful. If you are having problems with a figure, go over the instructions carefully. It is easy to read the instructions wrong, especially if they are complicated.

Caroline Extension

The Caroline extension is used in some of the figures in this collection that come from the Pacific Islands. The name refers to the Caroline Islands, foremost of which is the island of Yap. Despite the short instructions for this movement, it takes some practice to do it with ease. We add it here for reference. Don't worry about it

Caroline extension 1. Pick up upper thumb string from far side on index finger.

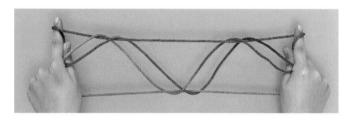

Caroline extension 2. Holding string firmly between thumb and straightened index finger, turn palms away from you to tighten strings.

now. You can practice it later, once you actually have done a figure that needs it.

1 Bend each index finger down and insert into the upper thumb loop from below, picking up far thumb string on the tip of the index finger (see Caroline extension 1).

2 Straighten the index fingers, keeping the loop just picked up as close to the tip of the finger as possible, held in place between the thumb and index finger. Turn palms away from you to tighten strings and display the figure (see Caroline extension 2).

The Caroline extension is used in Mr. Umake.

Beginning Figures

Here are some very simple figures to get you started. They come from places such as Africa and the Pacific Islands and the Arctic. Learn one and teach it to a friend.

Scissors

Level: Easy

**Loop Length: 36" or 40"
(91 or 102 cm)**

*This figure and its continuation, Tahiti
and Moorea, come from the island of
Tahiti.*

1 Do Opening A (see page 9 for
Opening A).

2 Pass thumbs away from you
under index loops and near little-finger
strings (a); return with near little-
finger strings (b).

3 Transfer index loops to thumbs
and release little fingers. There are
now three loops on your thumbs (c).

a

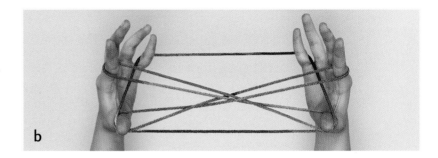

b

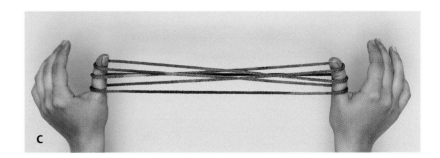

c

4 Hook index fingers down over the upper far thumb string (d), then down on the far side and back up on the near side of the two lower far thumb strings (e). Catch the lower thumb strings and extend index fingers.

5 Hook MRL fingers (remember, MRL = middle, ring, and little fingers) down over the two far index strings (f) and close them to palm.

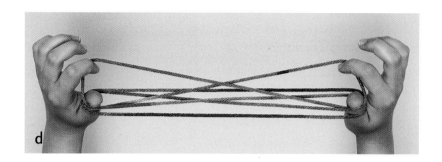

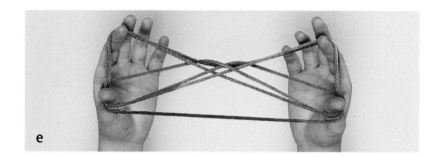

Scissors

6 Hold hands facing each other with thumbs at top and index fingers pointing away from you, to display g, Scissors.

7 Release thumbs from all loops and gently draw hands apart to display h, Tahiti and Moorea, neighboring islands.

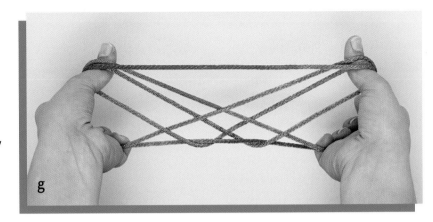

g

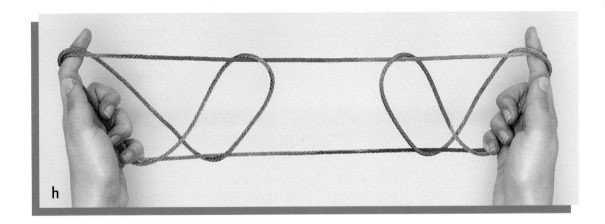

h

Level: Easy

Loop Length: 36" or 40" (91 or 102 cm)

This is probably the best-known string figure, aside from Cat's Cradle. It was made by many peoples of the world, including Native Americans, native Hawaiians, and West Africans.

1 Do Opening A.

2 Release the thumb loops and extend. You now have loops on your index and little fingers.

3 Pass thumbs away from you under all strings, then bring the thumbs back to their original position, carrying the far little-finger string on the backs of the thumbs (a).

4 Pass thumbs over the near index string, then under the far index string, and return to position with this string on the backs of the thumbs (b). Release the loops from your little fingers (c).

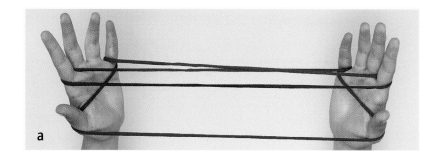

a

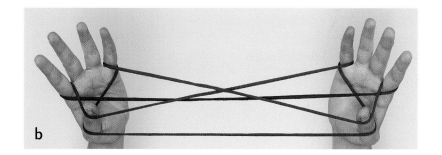

b

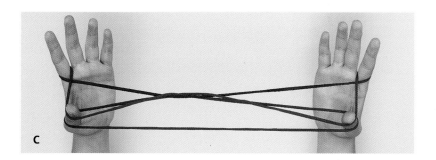

c

5 Pass little fingers towards you over the near index string and pick up the far thumb string from below (d). Return to position and release all loops from the thumbs (e).

6 Pass thumbs over index loop and into little-finger loop from below. Return with near little-finger string on the backs of the thumbs (f).

7 With left thumb and index finger grasp the right near index string, close to the index finger above the palmar string, and place it over the right thumb as well (g), so the loop is shared by the right thumb and index finger. Repeat with other hand.

d

e

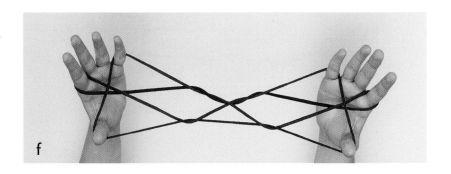

f

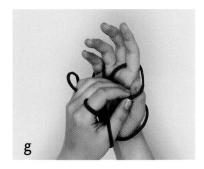

g

8 Navajo the thumb loops. Remember, this means to remove the lower of the two loops on a finger completely from that finger, passing it over the upper loop on that finger. You may find that this is most easily done with the fingers of the other hand.

h

9 The loop just navajoed wraps around the thumb loop, forming a triangular space. Dip each index down into the triangular space just below it (h). As you dip each index finger into its triangular space, turn your palms down and remove the little fingers from their loops. Extend the hands, turning your palms away from you. The index fingers are pointing up and the thumbs pointing down, with the figure extended between them. This completes Jacob's Ladder (i).

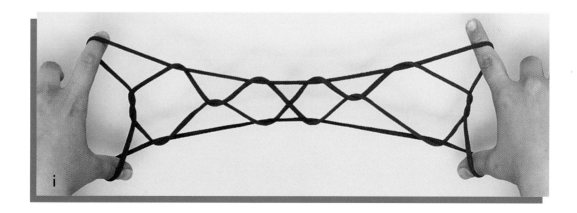

i

The following continuations of Jacob's Ladder can be made:

10 Locate the near index string that passes from one index finger to the other at the top of the figure. With your teeth, grab this string in the exact middle of the figure and pull it upwards (j). This makes the Eiffel Tower.

11 With the near index string still in your teeth, remove the index fingers from their loops and pull the thumb loops taut (k). This makes the Witch's Hat.

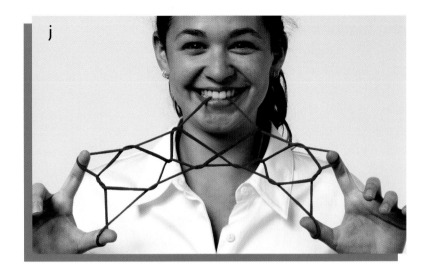

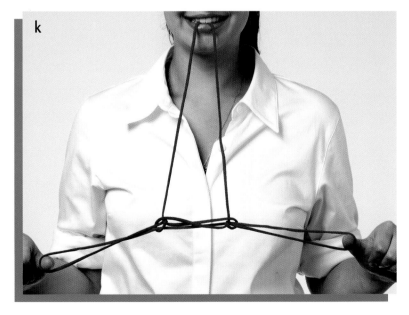

Level: Easy

Loop Length: 36″ or 40″ (91 or 102 cm)

This simple figure is from the Northwest Coast Kwakiutl Indians. The figure was also known to the Inuit, who called it Two Labrets. A labret is an ivory lip ornament.

1 Do Opening A. (See page 9 for instructions for making Opening A.)

2 Bend thumbs away from you over the far thumb string, then pass the thumbs under the index-finger loops and little-finger loops (a). Raise the thumbs on the far side of the little-finger loops.

3 Bring the thumbs towards you, picking up the far little-finger string on the side of your thumbs, until the thumbs are between the far index string and the near little-finger string. The far little-finger strings are still on the backs of the thumbs (b). (Or: pull the near little-finger string back over each thumb.)

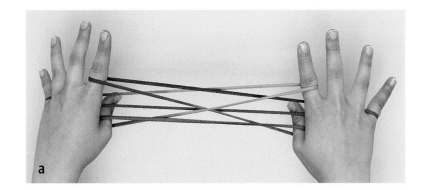

a

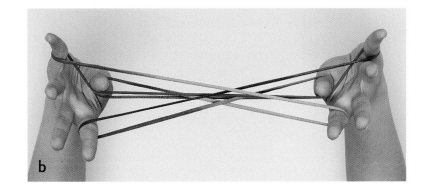

b

4 Now rotate the hands away from you, down, and up as in c, so that the thumbs are pointing up and the palms are facing you. The remaining fingers are pointing diagonally down. As you do this, the thumbs will pick up the near little-finger string.

5 Release loops from index fingers and extend (d).

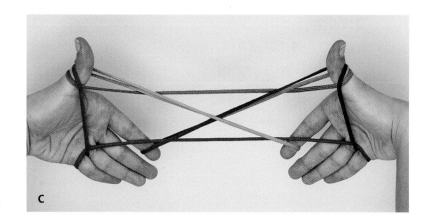

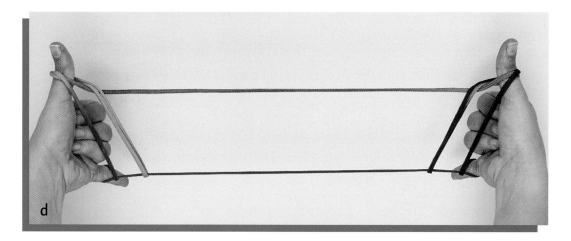

The Kwakiutl Indians would compete with each other in string-figure making. The winner was the person who could complete a figure the fastest.

Level: Easy to Medium

Loop Length: 54″ (137 cm) or longer

This is one of the more interesting figures because of the unusual placement around the neck. It comes from Papua New Guinea.

1 Place the doubled string loop around neck, with one loop longer than the other.

2 Insert hands from below into longer loop, as in Position 1 (a), and do Opening A (b).

3 Release little-finger loops, then pass the little fingers towards you over all loops, pick up from below the short neck loop, and return (c).

a

b

c

A Chest Ornament

4 Exchange index loops as follows: put the tips of your two index fingers together and move the loop on the left index finger onto the right index finger (d). Then, move the loop on the right index finger onto the left index finger, passing it over the loop previously transferred to the right index finger from the left index finger. Separate the hands carefully once this is done (e).

5 Pass right thumb and index from above through left index loop, remove the loop from the left little finger (f),

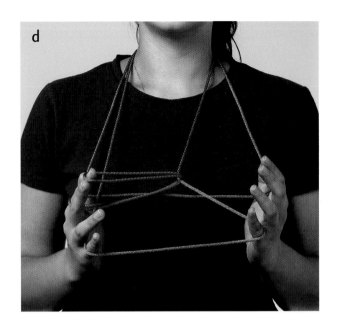

pull it up through the left index loop, and replace it on the left little finger without twisting it. Do this same procedure on the right hand, pulling the right little-finger loop up through the right index loop and replacing it on the right little finger without twisting it (g).

6 Release index fingers and thumbs from their loops, and with little fingers work figure down over chest (h).

Among the people of New Guinea, there were certain string figures that only men were permitted to make. Others, only women were permitted to make, and still others only married people were allowed to make. It was "tabu" (forbidden) to make string figures at night.

A Fishing Net

Level: Easy to Medium

**Loop Length: 40"
(102 cm)**

This very attractive figure is from Sierra Leone in West Africa. The figure was known from other parts of Africa as well, and similar figures are known from other parts of the world. Making A Fishing Net is not very hard, but if you use a loop that is too small, your fingers will be pretty crowded together during Step 7.

a

1 Do Opening A, picking up opposite palmar strings with middle fingers instead of indexes.

2 Transfer little-finger loops to ring fingers and thumb loops to index fingers, inserting fingers from below each time (a).

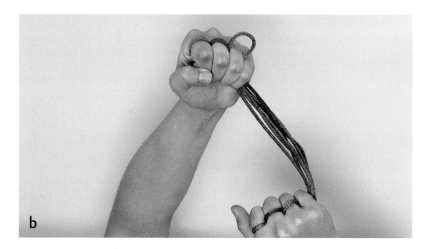

b

3 Make each hand into a fist, closing the fingers toward you and down over all strings to prevent slipping during the following movements.

4 With right thumb and index pull up the loop on the back of the left ring finger so it sticks up about an inch (b). Reach through this loop with the right thumb and index and pull the

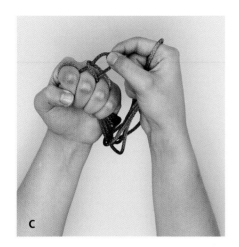

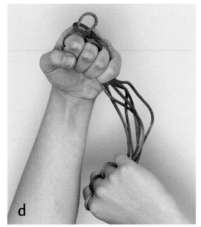

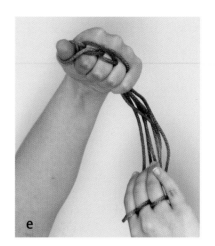

loop on the back of the left middle finger through the left ring-finger loop (c). Then pull the left index loop through the left middle-finger loop (d), and place this last loop pulled through on the left thumb, so that the left far thumb string is a continuation of the right near index string (e).

5 Repeat Step 4 with the right-hand loops. Open your fists, returning hands to normal position (f).

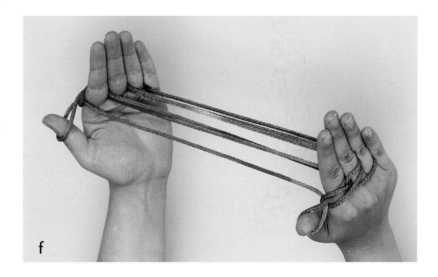

6   With palms facing each other, pass thumbs under the nearest transverse string (g) and navajo the thumb loops (h).

g

h

7 Repeat Step 6, working your way towards the little fingers, until all transverse strings have been picked up and navajoed. Make sure that as you work with each succeeding string, you pick up the same string with both thumbs.

8 When all strings have been navajoed, insert the little finger from above into the thumb loop of the same hand, release thumbs (i), and return little fingers to position. Extend hands to complete the figure, as shown in (j).

9 If you release the little fingers from their loops and extend your hands, you get back to the end of Step 2.

Lightning

Level: Easy to Medium

**Loop Length: 36" to 40"
(91 to 102 cm)**

This dramatic figure is known from both the Southwest Indians and Pacific Islanders. The method given here is from the island of Tonga.

1 Do the Index opening. (See page 11 for the Index opening.)

2 Pass thumbs away from you between upper and lower near index strings; pick up lower far index strings on backs of thumbs (a) and return.

3 Pass thumbs away from you over upper near index string; pick up upper far index string and return (b). You now have two loops on each thumb.

4 Bend middle fingers toward you and down over upper near index string (c); pick up lower near index string and return (d).

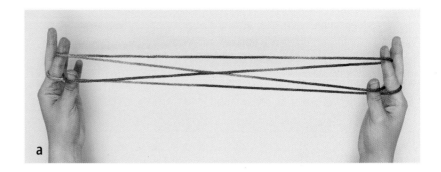

a

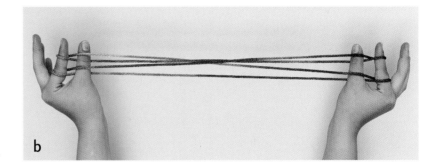

b

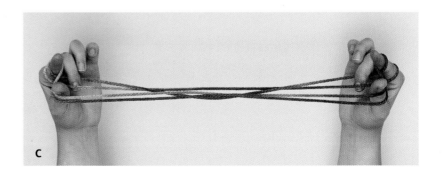

c

5 Each middle finger is in a small triangular space formed by a loop around the back of the finger and a palmar string across the front of the finger; the palmar string is seen to be the upper near index string (d). For each hand in turn, do the following: With the thumb and index of the opposite hand, take hold of the two strings in front of and in back of the middle finger, where they meet near the little finger (e). Withdraw the middle finger from the triangular space and reinsert it into the same space from above (f), which turns the strings away from you so that the near and far strings have switched position. Raise the middle fingers so they are once more pointing up.

d

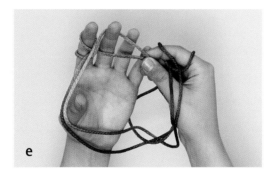

e

f

6 Repeat Step 5 to get g.

7 Press the thumbs down sharply onto the palmar middle finger string (h) to extend the figure (i). In the process, the original thumb loops will slip off. You can then release the thumbs and repeat this final movement as many times as you'd like.

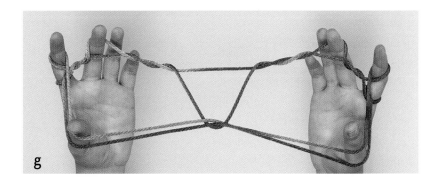

g

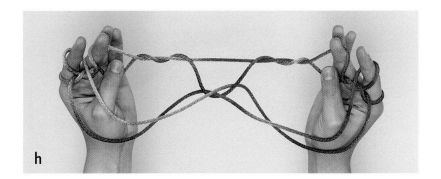

h

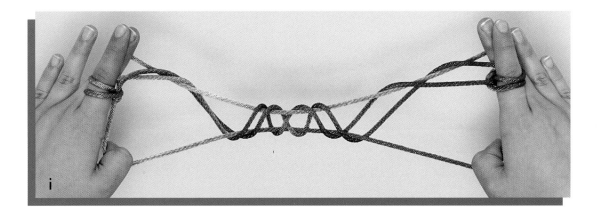

i

Now Try These

Here are some figures that are a little more difficult than the previous ones, but if you follow step by step, they won't be too difficult.

Hina's Skipping Rope

Level: Medium

**Loop Length: 40"
(102 cm)**

Here is another figure from the island of Tonga.

1 Do the Index opening (see page 11).

2 Rotate the upper right index loop a full turn away from you, as follows: Bring the hands together and with the left hand, grasp the strings of the upper right index loop close to the right index finger (a). Then circle the right index finger away, down, and towards you under its upper loop and back to position.

3 Pass thumbs away from you between upper and lower near index strings; pick up lower far index strings on backs of thumbs and return (b).

4 Pass thumbs away from you over upper near index string; pick up upper far index string and return. You now have two loops on each thumb (c).

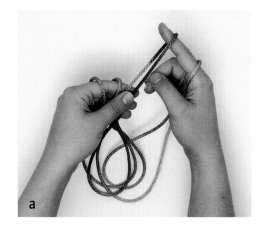

a

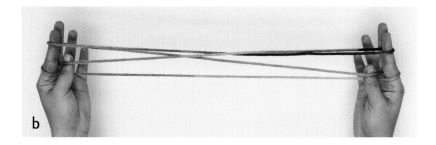

b

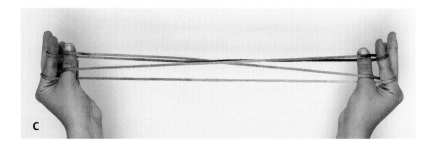

c

5 Bend middle fingers towards you and down over upper near index strings; pick up lower near index strings and return (d).

6 Each middle finger is in a small triangular space formed by a loop around the back of the finger and a palmar string across the front of the finger. The palmar string is seen to be the upper near index string (d). For each hand in turn, do the following: With the thumb and index of the opposite hand, take hold of the two strings before and in back of the middle finger, where they meet near the little finger (e). Withdraw the middle finger from the triangular space and reinsert it into the same space from above (f), turning the strings away from you so that the near and far strings have switched position. Raise the middle fingers so they are once more pointing up.

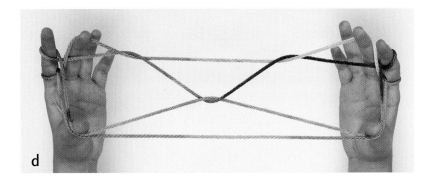

d

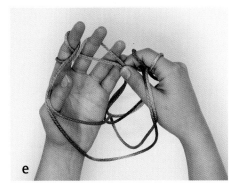

e

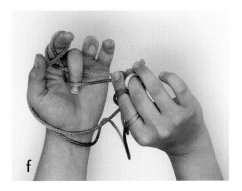

f

Hina's Skipping Rope

7 Repeat Step 6 (g).

8 Press the thumbs down sharply onto the palmar middle-finger string (h) to extend the figure (i). In the process, the original thumb loops will slip off.

The hanging string can be flipped over the figure from front to back, like a skipping rope. Keep everything on your fingers to do Teniako's Bridge.

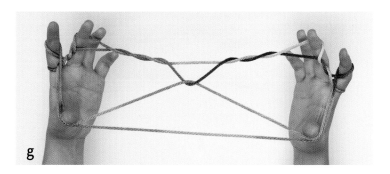

g

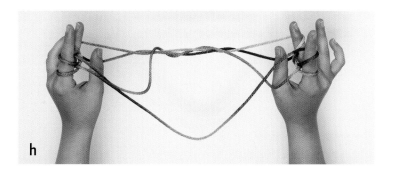

h

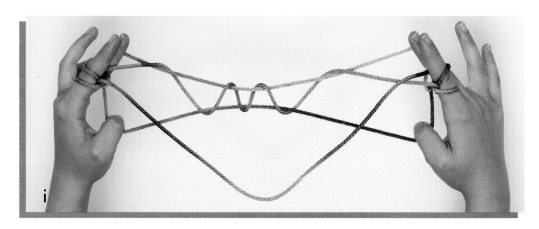

i

Level: Medium

Loop Length: 40″ (102 cm)

Teniako's Bridge continues from Step 8 of Hina's Skipping Rope.

9 Bring little fingers towards you and catch the loops held down by the thumbs (j). Remove thumbs from these loops. Insert thumbs from the back side of the figure into the loops now held down by the little fingers, catching the hanging string (k), and extend the figure by hooking the thumbs down and pulling tight. Let the strings slip off the little fingers. This makes Teniako's Bridge (l).

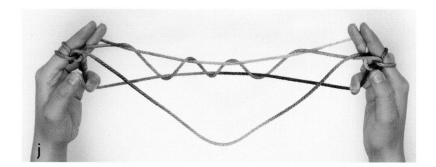

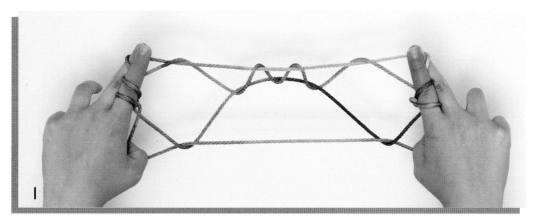

Ten Men

Level: Medium

Loop Length: 40″ (102 cm)

This figure is recorded from many different islands all over the Pacific.

1 Do Opening A.

2 Release the thumb loops and extend.

3 With the right thumb, hold down the right index loop (near and far string) and the near little-finger string. Bend the right index finger away from you over all strings, then catch up in the crook of the right index finger from below the far little-finger string (a). Straighten the right index finger back to its original position. You now have two loops on the right index finger (b).

4 Bring your hands together and insert the left index from below into the upper right index loop only (c).

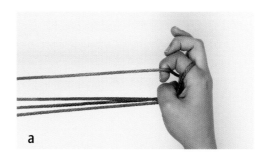

a

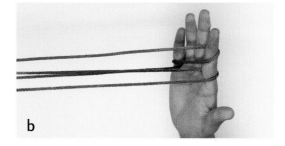

b

c

Extend hands, thus sharing the upper index loop. You now have one loop on each little finger and two loops on each index finger.

5 Pass thumbs away from you under index loops and into little-finger loops from below (d); pick up from below the near little-finger string on the backs of the thumbs and return to position.

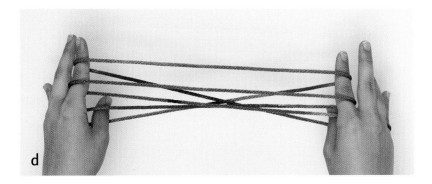

6 Share the upper index loops with the thumbs by inserting each thumb from below into the upper index loop on the thumb side of the figure only, and return thumbs to position (e). Navajo the thumb loops (remember, this means to move the lower thumb string up over the upper thumb strings and off the thumb entirely — see f).

7 Withdraw the index fingers from their upper loops only (g).

8 Transfer thumb loops to index fingers by inserting the index fingers from below into the thumb loops and withdrawing the thumbs from those loops.

9 Pass thumbs away from you under index loops (h) and into little-finger loops from below; pick up from below the near little-finger string on the backs of the thumbs and return to position.

10 Share the upper index loops with the thumbs by inserting each thumb from below into the upper index loop, and return thumbs to position (i). Navajo the thumb loops.

11 Bend middle fingers toward you over the upper far index string and pick up from below the lower near index string (j); return to position.

12 Release little-finger loops, turn palms away from you, and extend the figure as shown (k).

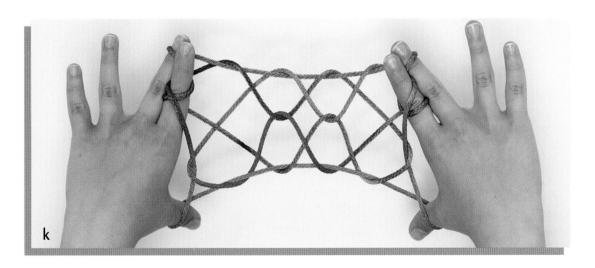

Crayfish

Level: Medium

Loop Length: 36″ or 40″ (91 or 102 cm)

This figure was made by a variety of methods, some very complicated, on several Pacific islands. The method given here, is by far the easiest. It comes from New Zealand.

1 Do Opening A.

2 Pass thumbs over index loops, then under little-finger loops, and return with both near and far little-finger strings (a).

3 Insert index fingers from below into thumb loops only, avoiding index loops (b), and return with far thumb string. Release thumbs. Extend. You now have two loops on each index finger and one loop on each little finger (c).

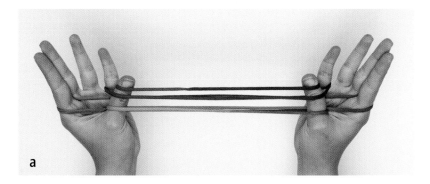

a

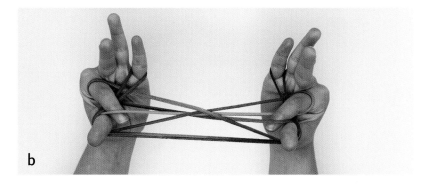

b

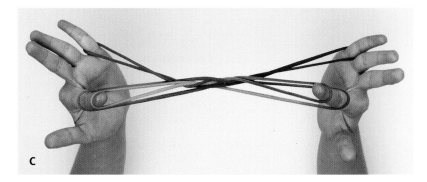

c

4 Pass thumbs from below through lower index loops and behind the upper far index strings (d), and hold the upper far index strings firmly against the index fingers with the thumbs. Then pull the index fingers down through their lower loops (e), towards you and up, allowing the lower index loop to slip off (f), and end up with previously held loops on index fingers. The effect of this movement is that the upper index loop is pulled through the lower index loop and turned over in the process. Although this (upper) index loop is held firmly between the thumbs and index fingers, the rest of the strings are held loosely (the hands are not extended).

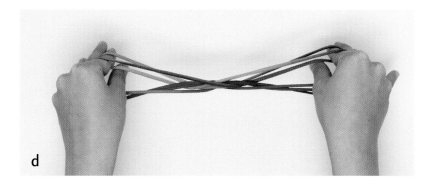

d

e

f

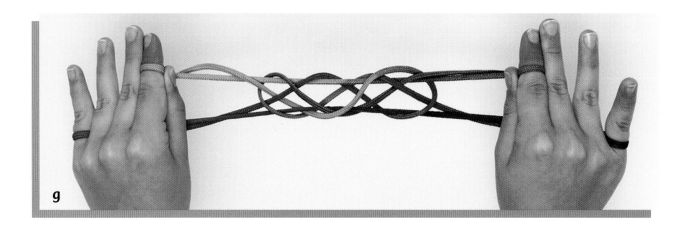

g

5 Press near index strings firmly against the index fingers with thumbs; turn palms away from you, and the figure appears (g).

STRING OLYMPICS

Some very challenging figures come from Nauru, an island in the Pacific. On Nauru, the craft of string-figure making was added into the island olympics, which was a regular competition held among the islanders that included model canoe-racing and kite-flying. Spurred on by the competition, the Nauruans experimented with string figures, with some spectacular results.

One competition was seen by an anthropologist early in the 20th century. He reported that the contestant would turn away from the audience while making the string figure, so they could not see how it was made, turning around to face the audience only when the figure was completed. In spite of this, the audience members would quickly attempt to reproduce the figure, often succeeding very quickly. Some figures took four people to construct and others took almost half an hour to complete!

String Figure Series

Although making individual string figures like those in the earlier parts of the book is rewarding, it is even more fun when you can move from one figure to another in a series. In traditional societies, the making of string figures was often accompanied by songs, chants, or stories. Try making up a story to go along with each series of figures given in this section.

Mr. Umake

Level: Medium

Loop Length: 36" or 40" (91 to 102 cm)

This is a series of three figures from the Gilbert Islands in Micronesia. Today the Gilbert Islands are a separate nation called Kiribati. You'll need a 36" (91 cm) loop to best display the final figure in the series. This series looks daunting at first because of the number of steps, but you will find that some of the steps are repeated several times, so it is not very hard to learn.

1 Do the Navajo opening.

2 Insert MRL fingers of each hand from below into index loops (a). Remember, MRL is an abbreviation for the middle, ring, and little fingers. Close MRL fingers over palmar string on index and MRL fingers and transfer the far index string to the thumb by inserting the thumb from above so the string slips off the index and MRL fingers and onto the thumbs (b); do not release the held string from the crook of the MRL fingers.

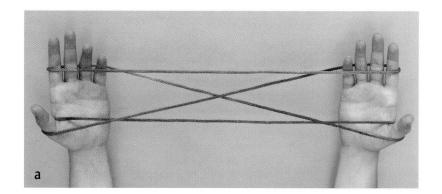

a

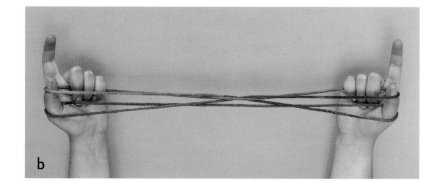

b

3 Insert index fingers from below and from the far side into the thumb loops that aren't held by MRL fingers and pick up the far thumb strings on their tips (c). Extend by turning palms away from you, pressing near index strings against index fingers with thumbs and continuing to hold on to the palmar string with the MRL fingers (this is basically the same as a Caroline extension).
This is d, Mr. Umake.

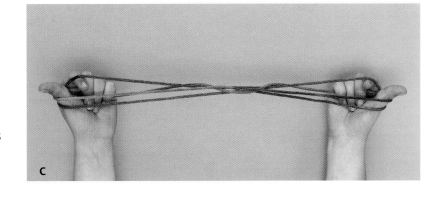

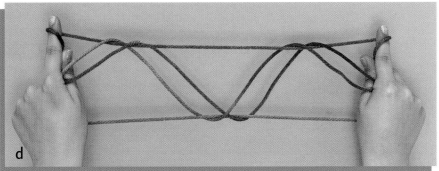

4 Release MRL fingers. Loosen thumb pressure on near index string and remove thumbs from index loops. Extend. You now have a loop on each thumb and a loop on each index finger (e).

5 Insert MRL fingers of each hand from below into index loops (f). Close only the MRL fingers over palmar MRL strings. Insert thumbs into far index strings so they slip off indexes and onto thumbs. Do not release string from the crook of the MRL fingers (g).

6 Caroline extension into far thumb strings, which results in a jumble of strings, as shown in h.

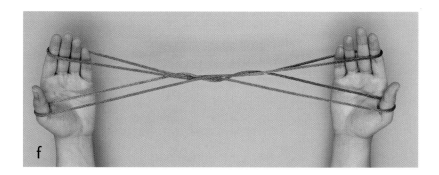

f

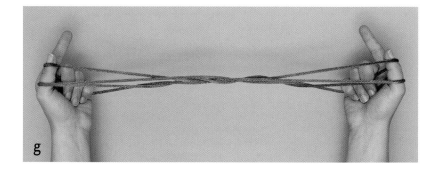

g

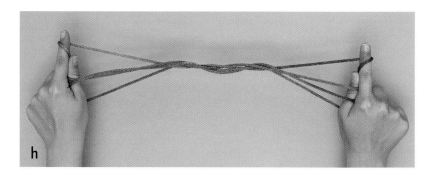

h

7 Take thumbs out of index loops and release MRL fingers (i). Repeat Step 2 (j and k).

8 Caroline extension into far thumb string, but with a twist: To extend the figure, you must turn the left hand with palm towards you and move it below the right hand; at the same time bend right hand so the palm is facing away from you. The figure (l), called Turning Over, is displayed vertically as shown.

9 Return your hands to their regular upright position, but keep all strings on fingers as in Step 8. Rotate the little fingers away from you (m) and up, releasing middle fingers, ring fingers, and finally the thumbs. You now have loops on each index finger and each little finger.

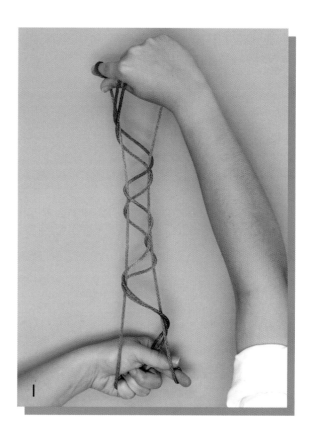

10 Pass thumbs under index loops and insert into little-finger loops from below (n); rotate thumbs away from you, down, towards you, and up, carrying with them the far little-finger strings. Release little fingers and return hands to position (o).

11 Insert MRL fingers of each hand from below into index loops. Close these fingers over the near index strings (p) and let the far index strings slip onto the thumbs (q).

n

o

p

q

12 Caroline extension into the top thumb loop (r). This makes s, A Swarm of Ants, which may require some arranging to display well.

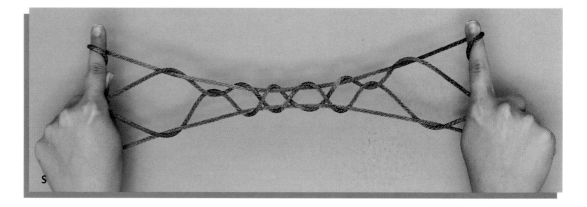

The natives of the Gilbert Islands, said to be "addicted" to string-figure making, would hold evening contests. An accomplished person would make figures and the assembled villagers would try to guess the identity of the figure.

Level: Easy to Medium

Loop Length: 40" or 54" (102 or 137 cm)

A long loop is needed for this sequence of figures from New Caledonia.

1 Do Opening A.

2 Push entire hands up through the index loops so these loops are around the wrists instead of the index fingers (a).

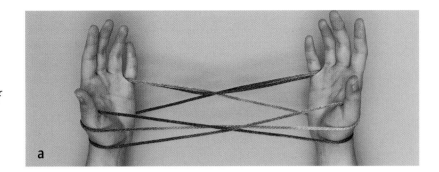

a

3 Insert thumbs from below into little-finger loops and return with near little-finger strings (b).

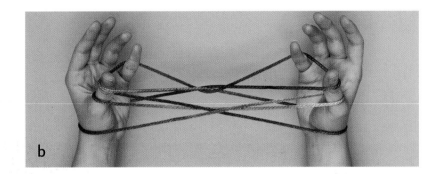

b

4 Insert little fingers from below into thumb loops and return with far thumb strings (c).

5 On each hand you have double loops shared by the thumb and little finger, and a single loop around each wrist. You now need to pull the wrist loop up through the double loop and place it on the index finger of the same hand. Here's how you do this:

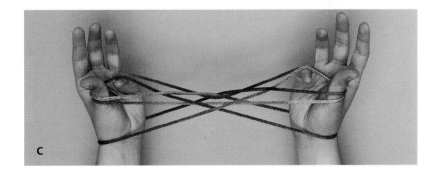

c

Crabs

With right thumb and index, lift double palmar loop off left hand (d). Slip the left hand out of its wrist loop (e) and with the left thumb and index push this loop from below through the palmar loops held by the right thumb and index (f).

6 Take hold of the former left wrist loop with the right hand, replace the double palmar loops in Position 1 on the left hand (g), then place the former wrist loop on the left index finger. Do the same movements with the right-hand palmar and wrist loops. Extend. This is h, Paths Among the Rocks for Little Crabs. Lean fingers inward a bit to display.

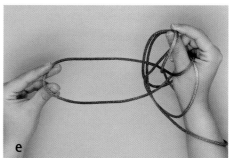

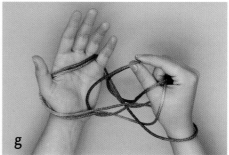

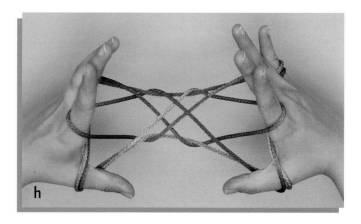

7 Insert right index finger from above through the index loop on the left hand; pick up on the index finger from below the double palmar strings and return to position (i), in the manner of Opening A. Repeat with left index finger on right hand.

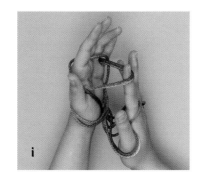

i

8 Navajo the single lower index loops over the double upper index loops on both hands. Pull hands taut; this makes j, A Hole for Crabs (k is a view of this figure from below).

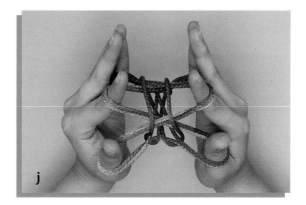

j

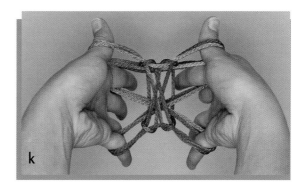

k

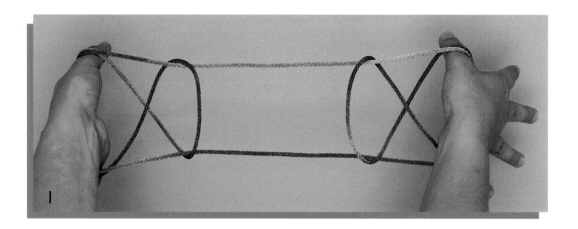

9 Release index finger loops and separate hands to get I, Crabs Running Off Into Holes.

HONOR C. MAUDE

Honor C. Maude devoted her life to gathering and studying string figures from the Pacific islands. Born in England, she first learned about string figures from a small book called *Cats Cradles from Many Lands,* by Kathleen Haddon (1911). In 1930, Honor Maude and her husband moved as newlyweds to the Gilbert Islands. The natives were very accomplished at string-figure making. She quickly became very fluent in the native language. In addition to learning string figures, she learned native arts and crafts such as basket-making and helped the natives learn to sell their crafts.

Because of the many years she spent collecting string figures and carefully describing how to make them, thousands of beautiful designs were preserved.

Level: Medium

Loop Length: 40" or 54" (102 or 137 cm)

This series comes from Japan, courtesy of Mr. Hiroshi Noguchi.

1 Do Opening A.

2 Pass thumbs away from you over near index string, then under far index string. Return thumbs to position with the far index strings on their backs.

3 Navajo thumb loops and release little fingers from their loops. Extend hands as shown. This makes a, The Sake Glass. Turn hands upright again.

4 Pass little fingers towards you over index loops. Pick up the far thumb strings on the backs of the little fingers (b), and return to position.

5 Bend index fingers down into their own loops, closing the index fingers over the palmar strings (c).

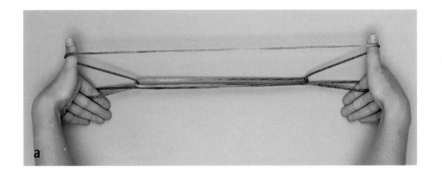

a

b

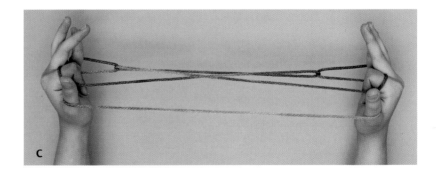

c

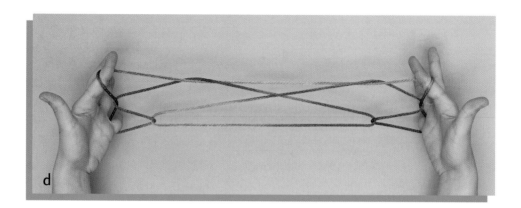

6 Then release the thumbs from their loops and raise the index fingers by rotating them towards you and up. This makes the figure called Two Mountains (d).

7 Bend thumbs down and pick up on the backs of the thumbs the segment of string in the middle of the bottom of Figure e. Release the index fingers from their loops. You now have loops on your thumbs and little fingers (f).

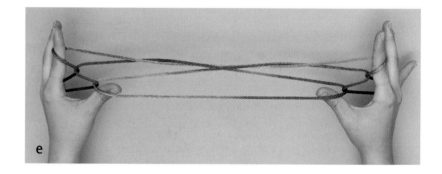

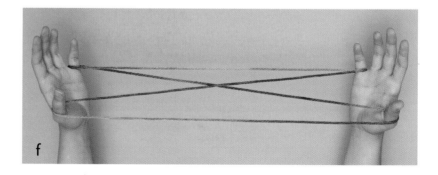

8 Insert index fingers into little-finger loops from below and return with the near little-finger strings on the backs of the index fingers (g).

9 Pick up on the backs of the middle fingers the palmar string on the opposite hand that runs between the index and little fingers, picking up with the right middle finger first (h). This movement is similar to Opening A.

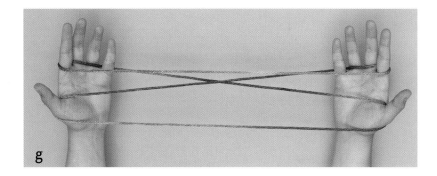

g

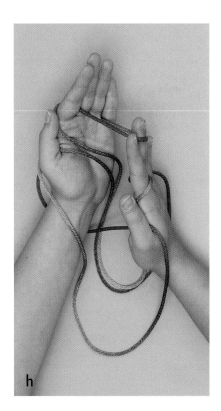

h

10 You now have loops on your thumbs, index fingers, middle fingers, and little fingers (i).

11 Pass little fingers towards you over middle finger and index loops, then bend them down and insert into the thumb loops from below. Pick up far thumb strings on the back of the little fingers (j) and return to position.

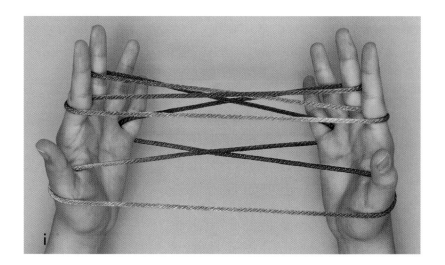

12 Bend index fingers down into their own loops, closing the index fingers over the palmar strings (k). Then release the thumbs from their loops and raise the index fingers by rotating them towards you and up. This makes the figure called The Butterfly (l).

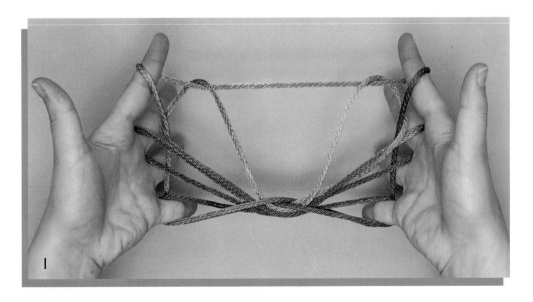

13 Pass thumbs away from you into the butterfly's wings and pick up on the backs of the thumbs the strings shown in m. Release the index fingers from their loops and extend. Be careful that the released index loops stay on the little fingers as upper loops. This makes n, Mt. Fuji, the famous Japanese landmark.

m

THE INTERNATIONAL STRING FIGURE ASSOCIATION

If you are really interested in string figures, there is an organization called the International String Figure Association (ISFA for short) that you can join. The ISFA was founded in 1978 in Japan. It is dedicated to preserving and teaching about string figures. The ISFA is now based in the USA, and there are members all around the world. You can find ISFA on the World Wide Web at http://www.isfa.org/.

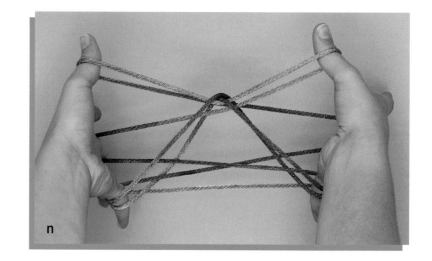

n

Figures for Two People

M aking string figures by yourself is fine, but the fun is doubled when you can get other people involved. Fortunately, there are a number of figures that can only be made by the combined efforts of two people. You've all heard of one such figure: the Cat's Cradle game. The figures in this section are just as much fun and the results are more spectacular.

A Mountain

Level: Medium

Loop Length: Two 36″ (92 cm) loops or one 36″ and one 40″ (102 cm) loop

The figure at the end of Step 6 has been reported from many Pacific islands. The final extension in Step 7 originates only in Hawaii. To make this figure requires two people. Each one needs a string.

1 Both players do Opening A.

2 With players facing each other, Player 1 inserts both hands from above into Player 2's index loops and returns with these loops on the wrists (a), removing them from Player 2's index fingers. Player 2 does the same movement with Player 1's index loops. Each player now has a loop on each thumb, each little finger, and around each wrist (b).

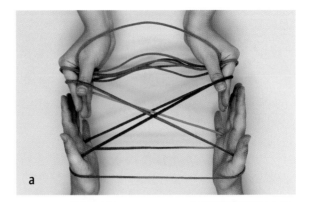

a

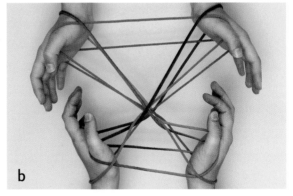

b

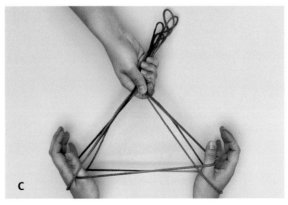

c

3 Player 1 removes hands from all loops, then gathers up the hanging strings (c) and wraps them two times around the strings held between Player 2's hands, turning towards Player 2's body first (d). Player 1 lets go of the ends of the wrapped strings.

4 Player 1, with right hand, removes the loop from Player 2's left thumb. Then Player 1 with left hand removes the loop from Player 2's left little finger (e).

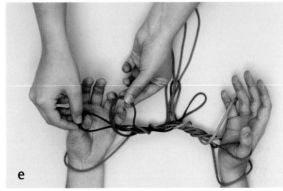

5 Player 2 releases his left hand from the wrist loop, then picks up Player 2's right thumb and little-finger loops with his left hand (f), removes his right hand completely from the wrist loop, letting go of it, and takes up in right hand Player 2's former little-finger loop. Player 2's left hand is still holding the right thumb loop from earlier.

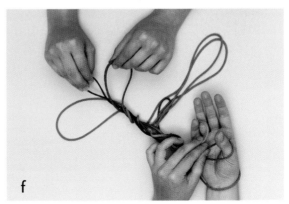

A Mountain

6 Both players draw hands apart until the strings in the center are unraveled and the symmetrical pattern in g appears in the center.

7 Player 1 releases the loop held in right hand. Both players pull the figure taut into the triangular shape shown. This is h, A Mountain.

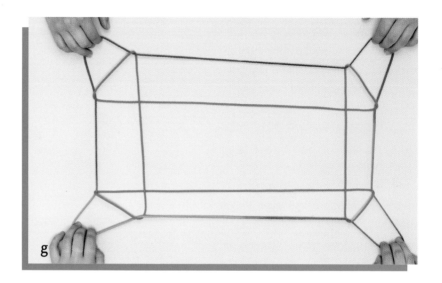

g

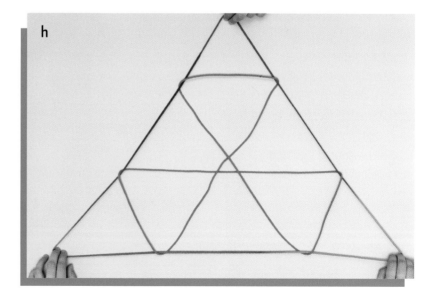

h

Level: Easy

Loop Length: Two 36″ (92 cm) loops or one 36″ and one 40″ (102 cm) loop

A Looking Glass and A Sting Ray were collected from the Patomano Indians of northern South America. Each requires two short loops of string. A second person is needed for the last step.

1 One person does Opening A, except she picks up the palmar strings with the opposite index and middle fingers, held closely together, acting as one finger (a).

2 Transfer little-finger loops to middle fingers, inserting middle fingers from below. Transfer thumb loops to index fingers, inserting index fingers from below. The result is seen in b.

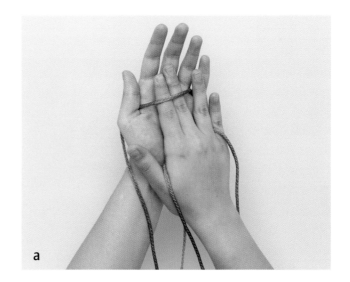

a

b

A Looking Glass

3 Next, Navajo the shared index/middle-finger loops over the single loops on index and middle fingers (c). However, do not simply drop the navajoed loop; keep it close to the palm of the same hand that the loop was originally on, and close the index and middle fingers of that hand over this string and into their own loops from above. Pull the navajoed string through the held finger loops on each index and middle finger. The old finger loops will slide off fingers (d).

4 Lay the figure made in Step 3 down and release from hands; arrange like Figure e.

c

d

e

5 Lay a second loop around the figure and draw a portion of this second loop through each of the four corner loops from underneath (f). With each hand, each person takes hold of the part of the second string that is through the first string loop and pulls the figure taut (g).

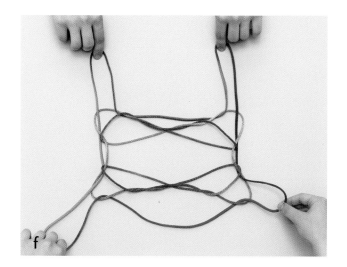

A Sting Ray

Level: Easy

**Loop Length: Two 36"
(92 cm) loops**

This figure was collected from the Patomano Indians of northern South America. Steps 1 to 6 are done by one person. The second person and loop are needed in Steps 7 and 8.

1 Hold one end of the loop in the right hand and bend the end of the loop down towards you. Insert left index and middle fingers towards you through the left and right spaces thus formed. You have a loop on the left index, a loop on the left middle finger, and a palmar string passes in front of the left index and left middle finger (a).

2 Repeat Step 1 using the other end of the long loop, placing the finger loops on the right middle and index fingers, making sure the strings that pass between the hands are parallel and do not cross.

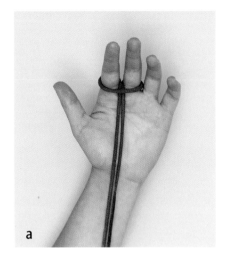

a

b

3 Bring left hand to right and with left thumb and index, pull up the loops on the backs of the right index and right middle fingers. Insert left index and left middle finger into the loops on the corresponding right hand fingers, passing the left-hand fingers from left to right (b) and remove right-hand fingers from those loops. There are now two loops on the left index finger and two on the left middle finger (c).

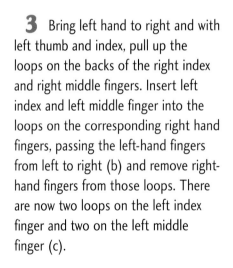

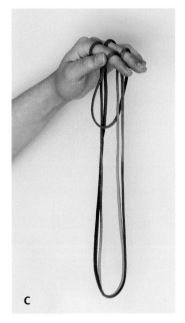

c

4 With the right thumb and index, pull up the lower left index and lower left middle-finger loops on the backs of the fingers and insert the right index and middle fingers, passing right-hand fingers from right to left into the corresponding left-hand loops just pulled up, as shown in Figure d.

5 With the right index and right middle fingers, transfer the raised loops from the left hand, slipping them over the front loops on the left index and middle finger, and extend hands (e).

6 Pull and wiggle the loop ends to tighten so that the loop in the center collapses to form a knot, as in f.

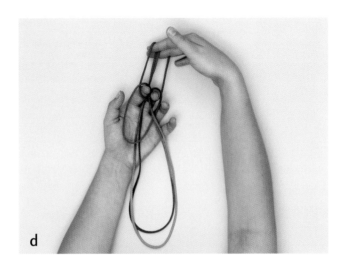

d

e

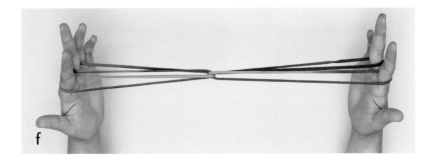

f

7 For this step you need the help of another person. Lay the figure down on a flat surface, without turning it upside down, and release from hands. Arrange the four loops as shown in g. Lay a second loop around the whole figure and insert a part of the second loop in the center of each of the four loops on the first string, inserting in loops from underneath (h).

8 Each person grasps two of the loop inserts of the second string within the four loops, grasping one in each hand, and pulls the figure taut. One hand pulls one loop longer to make the Sting Ray's tail (i).

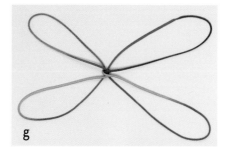

g

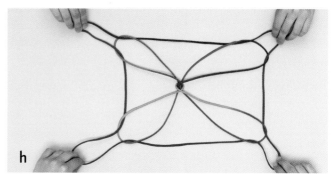

h

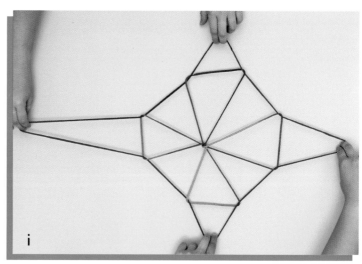

i

Catches and Tricks

S tring figures are all a bit magic, but there are some that are even more so than usual, because you can perform truly mystifying tricks with them. The ones in this section are the card tricks of the string figure universe. Here's a chance to truly amaze your friends!

Caroline Islands Catch

Level: Easy

Loop Length: 36″ (92 cm)

This catch was collected by W. H. Furness and published by his sister, Caroline Furness Jayne, in her 1906 collection of string games. It has also been recorded from many other Pacific Islands.

1 Put string in Position 1 on right hand only. With left hand, pull the right palmar string all the way to the left, over the hanging loop, which gets shorter, until you have tight loops around the right thumb and the right little finger with a palmar string passing under them (a). Repeat this same movement one more time (b), and put the long loop on the left hand in Position 1.

2 With left index finger, pick up the right palmar string from below and return.

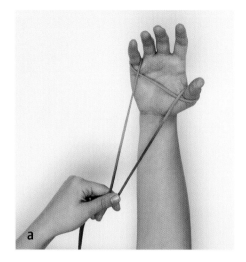

a

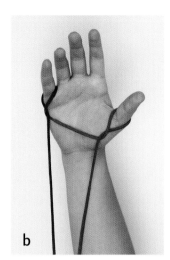

b

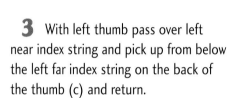

3 With left thumb pass over left near index string and pick up from below the left far index string on the back of the thumb (c) and return.

4 With right thumb pick up from below the right near little-finger string and return (d).

5 Pass left middle finger toward you and pick up from below the left near index string. Right now the left near index string is closest to your middle finger.

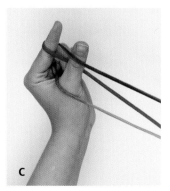

c

6 Pass right middle finger towards you and pick up from below the right far thumb string — the string that isn't palmar (see e).

7 Navajo the thumb loops, using the string that becomes the left palmar string but not the one that becomes the right palmar string. Be careful. If the figure doesn't turn out right, the most likely reason is that you navajoed the wrong strings in this step.

8 Release little-finger loops and extend the figure by turning the palms away from you and pulling the strings taut (f).

9 Once the figure is made, there are three diamonds. Ask another person to insert his hand into the central diamond. If you release all loops from your right hand and pull to the left, the strings will pull off the other person's hand, but if you release the loops from your left hand and pull to the right, he will be caught.

d

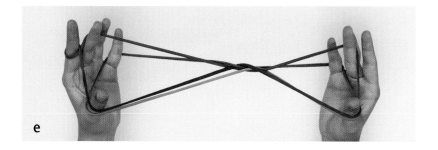

e

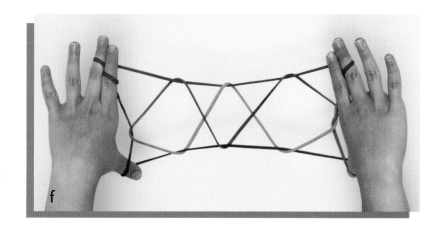

f

Cutting Off the Fingers #1

Level: Medium

Loop Length: 36″ (92 cm)

This trick is from the Kwakiutl Indians.

1 Hold the left hand with palm up and hang the loop across the four fingers so that there is a near index string, a far little-finger string, and a long loop hanging down behind (a).

2 With the right hand, grasp the strings that hang down behind the left hand, and bring them to the front side, passing the near index string continuation between the left index and middle fingers, and the far little-finger string continuation between the left little and ring fingers (b).

3 You now have a long loop hanging down over the left palm. With the right hand, grasp the two strings of this loop; then pass them both towards you between the left thumb and index, keeping the index string on top, around the left thumb and back away from you.

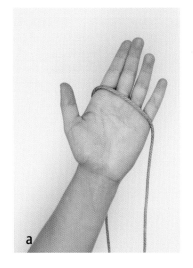

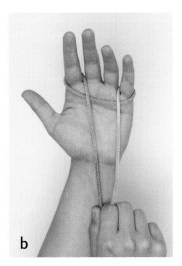

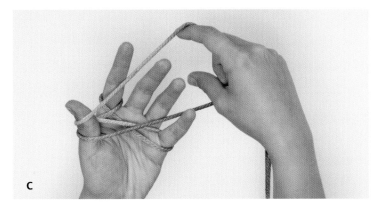

Pass each string of the loop to the back side of the left hand between the fingers from which it originated in Step 2 (c). Release right hand.

4 With the right thumb and index, grasp the string hanging down behind the left hand that passes between the left ring and little fingers and bring it around to the front of the left little finger (d). Pass the string across the palmar side of the four fingers and pass it to the back of the hand between the left thumb and index. Let go of the loop.

5 Insert right index from above into the two left thumb loops, remove left thumb, and pull right index away from left hand as far as you can. Let go of the loops.

6 Two loops (four strings) hang down on the palmar side of the left hand. Grasp all four strings in the right hand and pass them to the back of the left hand, passing all four strings between the left middle and ring fingers (e). Let go of strings with right hand (f).

7 With right thumb and index pull out the left lower palmar string. The string will come free from the left hand.

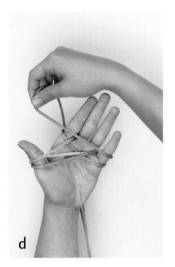

d

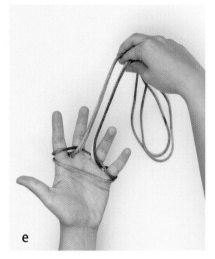

e

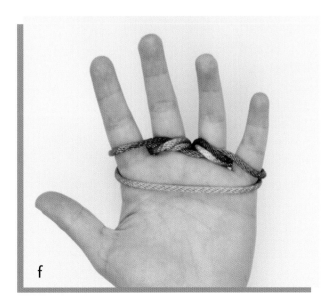

f

Cutting Off the Fingers #2

Level: Medium

Loop Length: 36″ (92 cm)

Here is another trick from the Kwakiutl Indians.

1 Hang the loop on the left thumb. With right MRL (middle, ring, and little) fingers, take hold of the hanging strings about 3″ (7.5 cm) away from left thumb.

2 From above, insert right thumb and index into loop hanging from left thumb and spread the fingers widely (a). Keep holding strings with right MRL fingers. Keep hands close to each other.

3 Rotate right hand a quarter turn away from you (thumb comes up), so that the left thumb strings are crossed. Bend left index down and pick up right far thumb string (from the far side), as shown in b.

4 Rotate right hand a quarter-turn towards you, back to its original position (c).

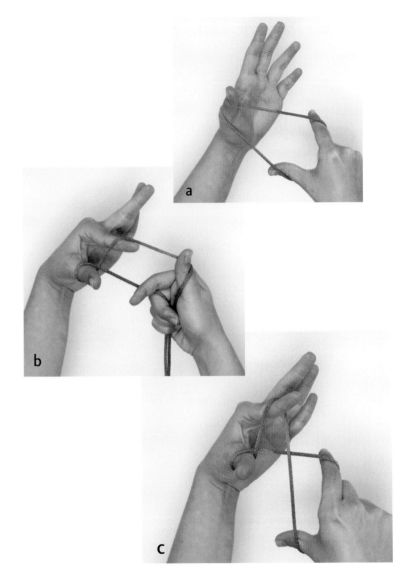

a

b

c

5 Bring left thumb over the right far thumb string and pick up from below the right near index string (d). Release all strings completely from the right hand and uncross the hanging loop.

6 Repeat the movements in Steps 2 to 4 twice more. You have the arrangement shown in e.

7 With right thumb and index, remove loops from left index (f). With the left thumb pointing up, pull the hanging loop to the right. The left thumb will come free of the loops around it.

8 If you experiment a little, you will notice this: You can repeat the procedure in Steps 2 to 4 as many times as you wish, but you must have an even number of loops (including the long hanging loop) around your left thumb for the loop to pull free of it in step 6. if you have an odd number of loops, the string will be caught on the left thumb.

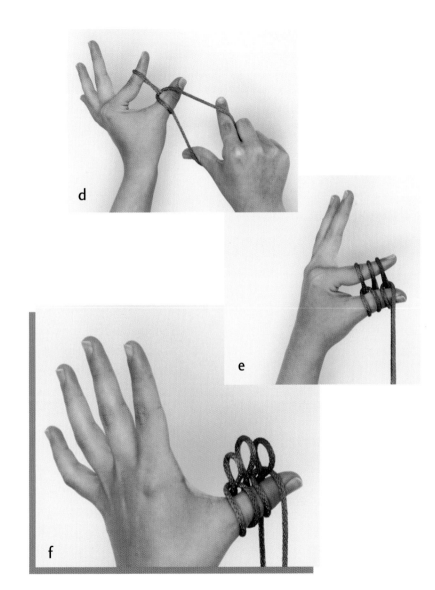

The Buttonhole Trick

Level: Easy

Loop Length: 36″ (92 cm)

This delightful trick from the Maori of New Zealand is probably my favorite of all string tricks. It never fails to amaze anyone who sees it. You should practice this until you can do it with no hesitation (for the most dramatic effect) before trying it on your friends.

1 Pass the string loop through a buttonhole, as shown.

2 Do Opening A.

3 Release the loops from both thumbs and extend (a).

4 Release the left index loop and right little-finger loop at the same time. The loop comes free of the buttonhole! It takes a little practice to let go of the correct strings in this final step, but it's not really that hard to learn.

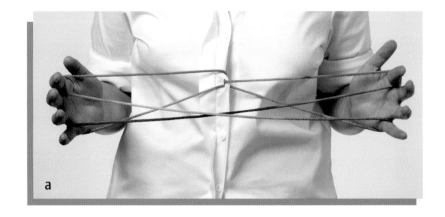

a

CAROLYN FURNESS JAYNE

Caroline Furness Jayne was one of the first authors of a book of string figures for a general audience. It was published in 1906. Some of the figures in our book came from Mrs. Jayne's collection. Caroline had help from her family. Her brother, William Henry Furness III, was a famous anthropologist in the early 1900s. At that time, anthropologists studying native cultures were the main collectors of string figures.

William Furness, along with Alfred C. Haddon, sparked Caroline Jayne's interest in this art form. Haddon helped develop the common terms used in describing how to make string figures.

Three-Dimensional String Figures

T hree-dimensional figures are the Corvettes of the string-figure world — flashy and elegant at the same time. Many of them are surprisingly easy to form.

Two Mountains and a Stream

Level: Easy to Medium

Loop Length: 36″ (92 cm)

Although fairly simple to make, this figure from the Inuit is a fairly realistic three-dimensional representation. It was also known to the Tlingit Indians of the Northwest Coast of North America.

1 Do Opening A.

2 Pass thumbs under index loops and pick up far index strings on backs of thumbs (a). Return to position and release index finger loops.

3 Transfer little-finger loops to thumbs from below. You now have three loops on your thumbs; keep them well separated (b).

4 Insert little fingers into lower and middle thumb loops from below (c) and hook down the transverse upper far thumb string, closing it to the palm with the little fingers (d).

a

b

c

5 With right index finger, pick up from below the upper near right thumb string (e). With left index finger, pick up the continuation of the same string that you just picked up with the right index — which is not the upper near string on the left side; it should be the central near string (f). Lift only this string entirely off thumbs (g), still keeping string on extended index fingers.

d

e

f

6 Navajo the thumb loops, which means you lift the transverse near thumb string off the thumb. Extend (h).

A VISIT FROM THE STRING SPIRIT

In Inuit mythology, there was a spirit of string figures, whose presence was signaled by the sound of crackling skins outside a hut. He was said to visit youngsters who overindulged in string-figure making at night and challenge them to a string-figure race, using his own intestines as a string. The child then had to make this figure over and over, as fast as possible, to drive the spirit away. If the child failed, the entire household would be unable to move. This story perhaps was told to youngsters to scare them into not goofing off at their chores.

Level: Easy

**Loop Length:
36″ loop (92 cm)**

This simple construction is from the Gilbert Islands, where it also was known as A Bed.

1 Do Opening A.

2 Release loop from left index finger.

3 Transfer left little-finger loop to left thumb from below (a).

4 Pass all left-hand non-thumb fingers (that is, the index finger, the middle finger, the ring finger, and the little finger) over both upper thumb strings and insert into lower thumb loop from above (b).

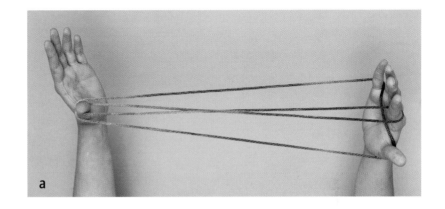

a

b

A King's Throne

Pick up the lower near thumb string on the backs of all four left-hand fingers, and remove the lower thumb loop completely from the left thumb, keeping it on the extended four fingers (c).

5 Transfer the loop on the four left-hand fingers to the left thumb, inserting left thumb from below (d).

6 Repeat Steps 4 and 5 twice.

7 Repeat Step 4 once more; then transfer the loop on the four left-hand fingers to the left little finger, inserting little finger from below (e).

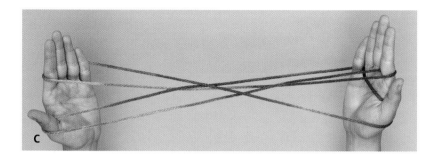

c

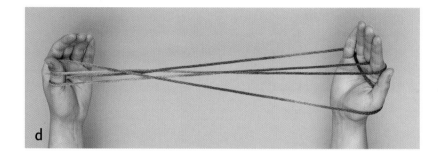

d

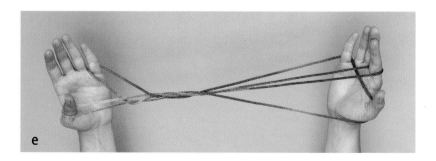

e

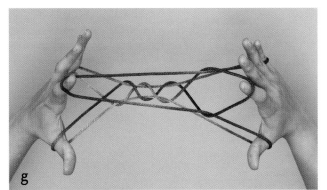

8 Insert left index finger through the right index loop and pick up from below the right palmar string (f) and return (g).

9 Release the right index finger and pull hands apart to display the final figure (h).

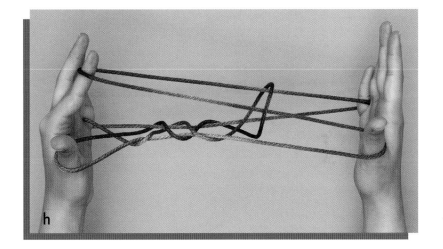

The Howler Monkey's Mouth

Level: Easy to Medium

Loop Length: 36" or 40" (92 or 102 cm)

This figure was collected from the Indians in Guyana, in the northern part of South America. They clearly knew some very inventive string figures.

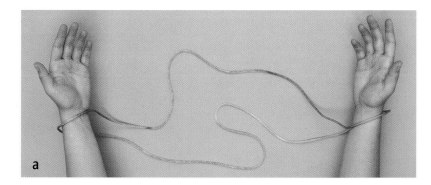

a

1 Put both hands into the loop so that it passes on the back of each wrist (a).

2 Grasping the strings near the middle with right thumb and index finger, pass the near string to the back of the left hand between the left thumb and index finger, and then to the front of the left hand between the left index and middle fingers. Pass the far string to the back of the left hand between the left ring and middle fingers, and then to the front of the left hand between the left index and middle fingers. This places a loop around the left index finger and the left middle finger (b). Let go of the strings you held with right hand but keep the loop on the right wrist in place.

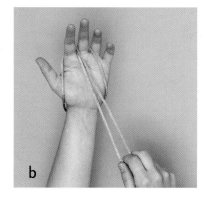

b

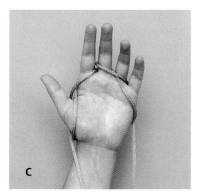

c

3 With the right hand, take the left far index string and place it between the left thumb and index finger, passing to the back of the left thumb. Take the left near middle finger string and place it similarly between the left ring and little fingers (c).

4 Pick up from below on right index and middle fingers the strings passing in front of the index and middle fingers on the left hand (see d). Separate hands. The wrist string is still around right wrist as well as left wrist.

5 Slip the left wrist loop over the hand and release it.

6 Transfer the right index and middle-finger loops to the same fingers on the left hand, inserting fingers from above (e). Navajo the left index and middle-finger loops.

7 Transfer the left index and middle-finger loops back to the same fingers on the right hand, and extend the figure (f).

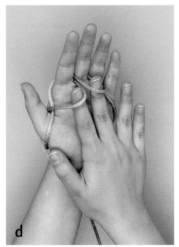

d

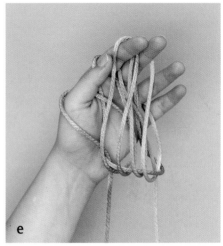

e

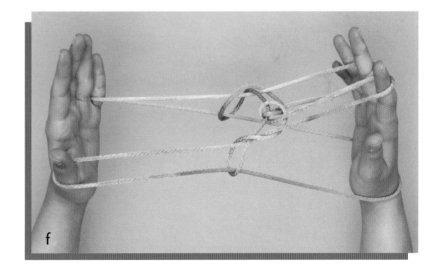

f

A Butterfly

Level: Medium

Loop Length: 36″ (92 cm)

This unusual and attractive figure comes from the Navajo Indians.

1 Do the Navajo opening.

2 With left hand, grasp right index strings several inches (6 or 7 cm) away from the right hand. Twist the right index loop by rotating the right index finger first toward you, then down (a) and under its loop, then away from you, and back up to position.

3 Twist the right index loop in the same manner as in Step 2, three more times, making a total of four twists in the loop (b).

4 Repeat the movements of Steps 2 and 3 with the left index loop and your right hand (c) and extend.

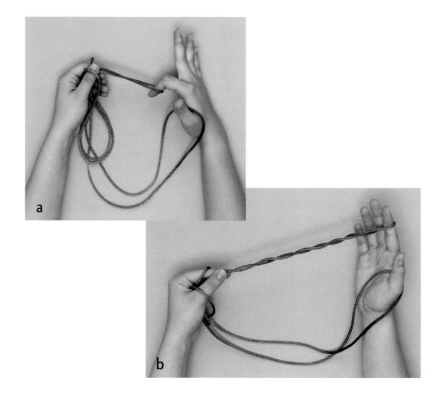

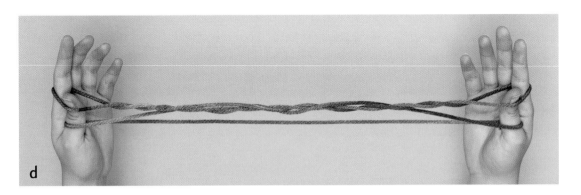

5 Insert thumbs from below into index loops and return with near index string (d).

6 Navajo thumb loops. The result is shown in (e).

7 Bring hands together and slip right-hand loops onto their respective left-hand fingers, releasing right hand completely from all loops (f). There are now two loops on the left thumb and two loops on the left index.

8 Transfer both loops on the left thumb to the right thumb by inserting the right thumb from below into the left thumb loops (g) and withdrawing the left thumb.

9 Transfer the left index loops to the left thumb by inserting the left thumb from below into the left index loops and withdrawing the left index (h).

f

g

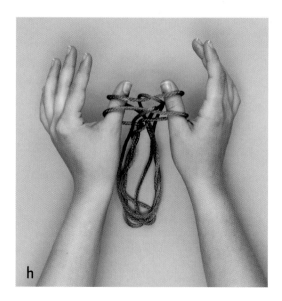

h

10 With both hands, insert MRL (middle, ring, and little) fingers from the far side into the thumb loops, extend a little, and close the MRL fingers over the strings (i). Then transfer the upper thumb loops to the index fingers from below and the far side and spread the fingers widely to display the Butterfly (j). The wings of the Butterfly are held up by the transverse index and thumb strings.

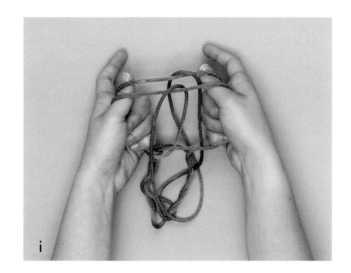

i

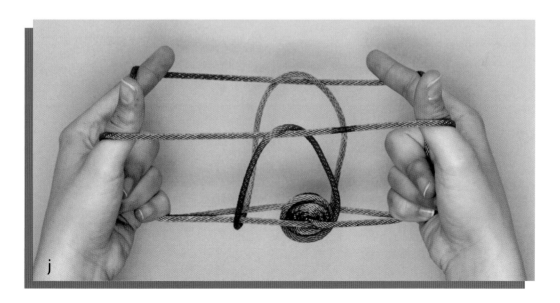

j

About the Author

Richard Darsie has been playing with string for almost ten years. His first experience of this art form came when his son's third-grade class learned how to do Cat's Cradle. He quickly learned that there were many figures that can be made by one person, and he began to explore them. These explorations led him to the local university library, where he devoured every string figure book and article available (there are a surprising number of these).

One of his favorite things about learning string figures is the strong feeling of accomplishment that comes with finally learning a complicated figure that has been struggled with for awhile. He is also particularly interested in the interesting stories about string figures from the native cultures where they originate.

In addition to string figures, Mr. Darsie's other main pastime is playing various kinds of music (folk, Renaissance, and Baroque) on several different instruments. He works as a Webmaster at the University of California at Davis.

Anderson, Johannes C., "Maori String Figures," *Memoirs of the Board of Maori Ethnological Research,* Vol. 2, 1927. Source of The Buttonhole Trick, A Crayfish.

Averkieva, Julia, and Mark A. Sherman, *Kwakiutl String Figures,* University of Washington Press, Seattle, 1992. Source of Cutting Off the Fingers #1, Cutting Off the Fingers #2, and Walking Sticks of an Old Woman.

Compton, R. H., "String Figures from New Caledonia and the Loyalty Islands," *Journal of the Royal Anthropological Institute,* Vol. XLIX, pp. 204-236, 1919. Source of Crabs.

Dickey, James, "String Figures From Hawaii," *Bulletin of the Bernice P. Bishop Museum,* Vol. 84, pp. 763-901, 1941. Source of A Mountain.

Hornell, James, *String Figures from Fiji and Western Polynesia,* Bernice P. Bishop Museum, Bulletin No. 39, Honolulu, 1927. Source of Lightning and Scissors/Tahiti and Moorea.

Hornell, James, "String Figures from Sierra Leone, Liberia, and Zanzibar," *Journal of the Royal Anthropological Institute,* Vol. LX, pp. 81-114. Source of A Fishing Net.

Jayne, Caroline Furness, *String Figures and How to Make Them,* Dover Publications, 1962; originally *String Figures,* Charles Scribner's Sons, 1906. Source of A Butterfly, Caroline Islands Catch, Jacob's Ladder, Ten Men, and Two Mountains and a Stream.

Maude, Honor C., "String Figures from Tonga," *Bulletin of String Figures Association,* No. 13, pp. 7-21, 1986. Source of Hina's Skipping Rope and Teniako's Bridge.

Maude, Honor C., and H. E. Maude, *String-Figures from the Gilbert Islands,* Memoir No. 13, The Polynesian Society, 1958. Source of A King's Throne and Mr. Umake.

Maude, Honor, and Camilla H. Wedgwood, "String Figures from Northern New Guinea," *Oceania,* Vol. XXXVII, pp. 202-229, March 1967. Source of A Chest Ornament.

Noguchi, Hiroshi, "String Figures of Japan 1," *Bulletin of String Figures Association,* No. 7, pp. 1-21, 1982. Source for Mt. Fuji. Used by permission.

Roth, W. E., "String Figures, Tricks, and Puzzles of the Guiana Indians," In *38th Annual Report of the Bureau of American Ethnology,* pp. 500-550, 1924. Source of The Howler Monkey's Mouth, A Looking Glass, and A Sting Ray.

Index

Butterfly, 61, 90
Buttonhole Trick, 80
Caroline extension, 12
Caroline Islands Catch, 74
Chest Ornament, 23
Crabs, 53
Crayfish, 42
Cutting Off the Fingers, 76, 78
Eiffel Tower, 20
extend or extend hands, 8, 9
Fishing Net, 26
from above and from below, 7
Hina's Skipping Rope, 34
Howler Monkey's Mouth, 88
Index opening, 11
index finger strings, 5
International String Figure Assn., 62
Jacob's Ladder, 18
Jayne, Caroline Furness, 80
King's Throne, 85
Lightning, 30
little-finger strings, 5
Looking Glass, 67
loops: loop lengths, 5; lower and upper loops, 6; navajoing loops, 7; sharing a loop, 8; transferring a loop, 8
lower and upper loops, 6
Maude, Honor, 56

Mountain, 64
Mr. Umake, 46
MRL fingers, 6
Mt. Fuji, 57
Navajo opening, 10
navajoing loops, 7
Opening A, 9
palmar string, 6
Paths Among the Rocks for Little Crabs, 54
Position 1, 8
return to position, 7
Sake Glass, 57
Scissors, 14
share a loop, 8
Sting Ray, 70
string positions, 5
Swarm of Ants, 52
Tahiti and Moorea, 16
Ten Men, 38
Teniako's Bridge, 37
thumb strings, 5
transfer a loop, 8
Turning Over, 50
Two Mountains, 58
Two Mountains and a Stream, 82
Walking Sticks of an Old Woman, 21
Witch's Hat, 20